A NOTE TO PARENTS ABOUT BEING BOSSY

Nobody likes to be bossed around. Giving into a bossy person runs counter to human nature. Most people do not want to relinquish control of their lives to someone else. Therefore, it is normal and even healthy when children resist being bossed by another person.

The purpose of this book is to define bossy behavior. It is also to encourage children to avoid being bossy and to avoid being bossed.

There is usually at least one person in every situation who wants his or her own way all of the time. These people often try to bribe, threaten, and even scare others into submission. In order for your child to stand up to these people, he or she needs to know that it is acceptable to question commands coming from another person. It is also acceptable to expect that every person, including your child, is entitled to have his or her own way some of the time.

This book belongs to:

_____

No part of this publication may be reproduced in whole or in part, or stored in
a retrieval system, or transmitted in any form or by any means, electronic, mechanical,
photocopying, recording, or otherwise, without written permission of the publisher.
For information regarding permission, write to: Scholastic Inc.,
Attention: Permissions Department, 557 Broadway, New York, NY 10012.

Published by Scholastic Inc.
90 Old Sherman Turnpike, Danbury, CT 06816.

SCHOLASTIC and associated logos are trademarks and/or
registered trademarks of Scholastic Inc.

ISBN 0-7172-8594-4

First Scholastic Printing, October 2005

A Book About
Being Bossy

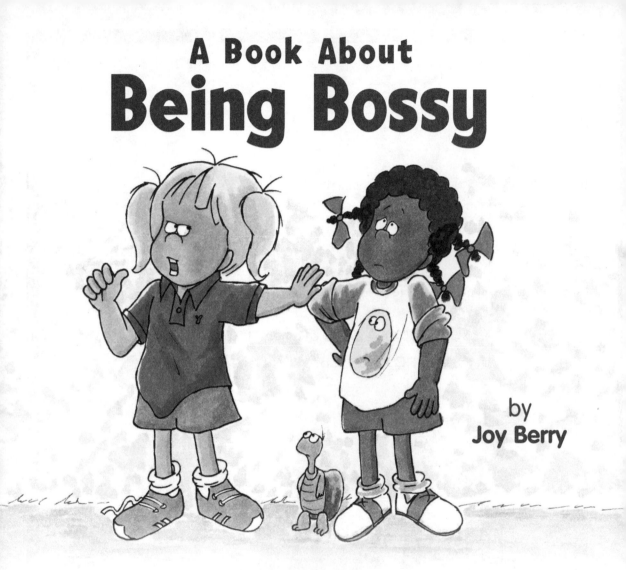

by
Joy Berry

SCHOLASTIC INC.

New York   Toronto   London   Auckland   Sydney
Mexico City   New Delhi   Hong Kong   Buenos Aires

This book is about Katie and her friend Tami.

Reading about Katie and Tami can help you understand and deal with **being bossy.**

Bossy people want to have their way all the time.

Bossy people think they know what is best for everyone. They think they know what everyone should do.

Bossy people like to tell others what to do.
They expect others to obey them.

Sometimes bossy people try to *bribe others.*

They promise things to get people to obey them.

Sometimes bossy people try to *threaten others.*

They say they will go away or not play if people do not obey them.

Sometimes bossy people try to *frighten others.*

They act as though they might hurt the people who do not obey them.

Most people want to have their own way some of the time.

They do not want others always telling them what to do. They do not like to be bossed.

If you are like most people, you do not want to be bossed. It is important to treat other people the way you want to be treated.

If you do not like being bossed, you must not be bossy.

Try not to be bossy. Remember that it is not fair for you to have your way all the time.

Take turns choosing what to do when you are with someone else. Let the other person choose one activity, and you choose the next.

Select an acceptable activity when it is your turn to choose. The activity should be:
- safe,
- something your parents allow you to do, and
- something that everyone can enjoy.

Be a good sport when others have their turn to choose an activity. Do what they choose if the activity is safe and something your parents allow you to do.

Try not to complain when others choose an activity. Do whatever you can to make the activity enjoyable for everyone.

Try not to be bossy. Do not bribe, threaten, or frighten anyone into obeying you.

No one likes to be bossed. If you do not
want to be bossed, you must not be bossy.